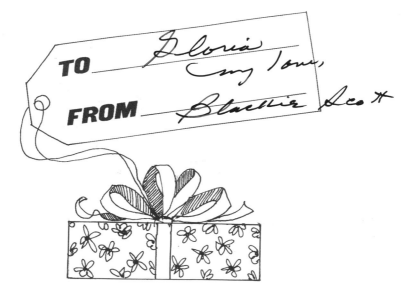

TO _____ Gloria
_____ my love,

FROM _____ Blackie Scott

Published by
Peachtree Publishers, Ltd.
494 Armour Circle, NE
Atlanta, Georgia 30324

An earlier version of this work appeared in 1988.

Book and cover design by Terri Fox

10 9 8 7 6 5 4 3 2

Manufactured in Mexico

ISBN 1-56145-112-6

Library of Congress Catalog Number 88-61460

Retire & Rejoice

Blackie Scott

Illustrations by Bill Johnson

PEACHTREE
ATLANTA

Dedicated with love to
my Jack
(the most patient retiree in the world)

·CONTENTS·

" *You better believe we're independent!*"

· 1 ·

RETIREMENT
(Let's Hang It Up)

"Retirement" is that word we've all heard since we picked up our first paycheck. Sometime, someday...and now, here we are, facing this unknown. Not only do we face retirement; now the world knows just how old we are! Don't despair. I have found the secret to staying young. Eat sensibly, work hard, worship regularly, and lie about your age! It is acceptable behavior to celebrate the same birthday again and again and again.

In this century, we have gained 26 years of longevity. These "bonus years" can, and should be, fulfilling and fun.

This book is written in hopes that you will see a bit of yourself in it and laugh. Many situations were prompted by "on-hand experiences" from friends; and, I must confess, I've been a covert observer of the world of seniors.

Don't forget to oil the wheels on that rocking chair, for you are going places! Where? I'm sure you don't have the answer, nor do I; but it will be fun.

Relax! Enjoy!

"Now, what are we going to do with our day?"

As the wife of a retiree and a friend of many, I'm sure the key to happiness is attitude. Dr. Norman Cousins has proved that laughter can actually change our physical being. Following a hearty laugh, beta endorphins are released into our bodies, promoting healing and a sense of well-being. Now, really, if a good "belly laugh" is equivalent to a pill, save your money!

If you are too busy to be miserable, you will be happy.

"Now, Mildred, relax! Remember, we're retired!"

Retiree, musing over his forty-year watch: "I wonder why a gold watch *now*, when time is suddenly so unimportant!"

One retiree was the eternal optimist. He was always in a good mood, sitting on GO for any activity. "Worry over the future" was not even in his vocabulary. Asked his secret, he replied, "Live for today. I don't even buy green bananas!"

A retired husband is a wife's full-time job.

I'm saving that rocker for
the day when I feel as old as I really am.
—Dwight D. Eisenhower

Following a very lavish celebration at a retirement dinner, the guest of honor made this remark: "I'm not retiring out of a job. I'm retiring into life."

Before   *After*

You do not have to teach the paths of
the forest to an old gorilla.

"Darling, I said give a hint of your figure, not a detailed blueprint!"

ADJUSTMENTS
(Don't Call the Chiropractor)

You reach a point in life when, although you have
not officially joined the retirement ranks,
you have many in your circle of friends who have.
You become aware through these friends that
retirement cannot be taken for granted.

There are adjustments, surprises, and many rewards.
I have daily reminders of these experiences.
They are shared, usually secretly, by the retired couple.

Let's face it, we're in this together! A sense of humor and respect for each other will carry us through these years.

It's not the years that make us grow, but the changes— and it's the changes, not the years, that matter.

❧

Age is a matter of mind.
If you don't mind, it doesn't matter.

❧

I heard someone say,
"Growing older is a journey from
passion to compassion."

Overheard following a presentation to a group of seniors—
(this senior has all the answers):
Rule #1—Never lay your wallet or your glasses down, anywhere, anytime!

❧

Just let me call you "Sweetheart"—
I can't remember your name!

❧

At our age, Happy Hour is a nap.

*I'm amazed at the number of persons starting a second career
after retirement, and the scores who never retire.
To quote:*

Barbara Cartland, writer:
"I think old people are so much better
when they have something to do. Nobody yet
has ever been known to die from overwork." [1]

*Art Linkletter, TV personality, author,
humorist, and lecturer:*
"It takes guts to grow old." [3]

Alice Faye, former movie queen:
"It's been over 25 years since I made my last film, but the old rocking chair hasn't got me yet." [4]

The great George Burns:
". . . fall in love with what you're doing for a living." [2]

He did; and we've stayed in love with him.
You really do send out a special energy to all ages as you face life with a smile.

I've read that Bette Davis had a pillow in her
house with the words "Old Age is Not for Sissies."

❧

Bumper sticker:
Avenge Yourself: Live Long Enough
To Be a Problem To Your Children.

❧

Middle age is when you're sitting home on Saturday
night, the telephone rings, and you hope it isn't for you.
—*Ogden Nash*

"*He's suddenly decided you're* not *too expensive!*"

After cajoling her husband for forty years to go to church, she finally gave up. Recently, she noticed his dialogue was

different: "I'm going fishing, God willing." This new phrase was automatically added at every opportunity. She candidly asked, "Why are you suddenly adding 'God willing?'" His sly response was, "Well, just in case you're right, I thought it's about time I make a few points."

I used to burn, but now I smolder;
I used to boil, but now I simmer.
Is this getting older or better?

❧

Two of my favorite decorative pillow tops:

Youth is a gift of nature.
Middle age is a work of art.

Age and treachery
will overcome youth and skill.

"For some reason, I feel it's not the modest anniversary gift the children have in mind."

·3·

ATTITUDE

(Trust Me, Have I Ever Been Wrong?)

The key to successful retirement is A.A.
No, not what you're thinking!
Activity and Attitude!

✺

Don't let this be said of you: "Your mind is like concrete—thoroughly mixed and permanently set!"

✳

Leisure is a beautiful garment, but it will not do for constant wear.

✳

To fill the hour, that is happiness.
—*Ralph Waldo Emerson, "Experience"*

"What do you mean—no reason to shave?"

It takes the combination—rain and sunshine—
to make a rainbow.

☀

Nothing is really work unless you
would rather be doing something else.

Those who think they know it all
are very annoying to those of us who do.

✳

Don't take life too seriously—
you'll never get out of it alive.
—*Bugs Bunny*

✳

Bumper sticker:
When We Are Over the Hill,
We Pick Up Speed.

Better to remain silent and be thought a fool
than to speak and remove all doubt.
—Abraham Lincoln

✺

By swallowing evil words unsaid,
no one has ever yet harmed his stomach.
—Winston Churchill

Sometimes it takes a lot of thought...and effort...
and downright determination to be agreeable.

☀

This store owner really knows his customers.
Sign in large Florida convenience store:
Call home now!
Save a trip. What did you forget?

"I know it's the third of the month...but today's a holiday!"

*Two retirees were "cooling it" in a small town jail,
following a sentence for fishing out of season.*

First fisherman: "That's really a stiff sentence,
and we did have our licenses!"

Second fisherman: "Don't worry,
we'll be out in no time.
My wife hasn't let me finish
a sentence in forty years!"

I have learned so much since I was seventy years old;
more within the last ten years than any other decade.
Why should I quit?
—Pearl S. Buck

✻

One should never trust a woman who tells her age.
A woman who would tell that would tell anything.
—Oscar Wilde

To me, old age is ten years older than I am.
—*Bernard Baruch*

✺

My favorite antiques are my old friends.

✺

Telling his Kentucky voters why they should elect him
U.S. Senator, Alben W. Barkley said, "I'm old enough to
know how, and young enough to do it."

I will tell you that my age varies according to the day and the people I happen to be with. When I'm bored, I feel very old; and since I'm extremely bored with you, I'm going to be 1,000 years old in five minutes if you don't get the heck out of here at once!
—*Gabrielle "Coco" Chanel, to a reporter*

❋

Age isn't important unless you're cheese or wine.

"He'll be right over with the ladder—
just watching some silly ball game."

•4•

LAUGHTER

(Your "Funny Bone" Is the Key to Good Health)

Will Rogers is quoted as saying, "We are all here for a spell; get all the good laughs you can."

Humor is golden—and if it provokes laughter, it's magic. For many of us, it is a natural reaction; to some, a learned response.

A famous lieutenant commander in the navy retired.
His wife was known for her sunny personality and
love of people, but her house was not "ship shape."
A clean house meant a swept step as you entered,
a cleared chair for you to sit in, and a clean cup
for your coffee. After several months of
"adjustment," her husband commented,
"One of the advantages of living in an unstructured home
is that we are constantly making exciting discoveries."

My dears, the lieutenant commander had to find
humor, or he would have returned to the ship.
I think she must have penned this:
"Dull women have immaculate houses."

The man who can smile when things go wrong has thought of someone to blame it on.

❀

A hearty laugh is a workout for our internal organs— jogging *inside*!

The classic joke teller at "The Club" had a unique style.
His stories were never rambling, always brief—
a short pause, then the punch line.
Usually, he walked away as his friends
held their sides in laughter.

His reason for this style:
"If I stretch it out too long, my audience
has time to think of one to tell me."

❀

You know you're getting old when the
candles cost more than the cake.
—Bob Hope, at one of his birthday parties

❀

If I'd known I was going to live so long,
I'd have taken better care of myself.
—Eubie Blake

Money cannot buy happiness,
but it buys the kind of misery we enjoy.

❀

Laugh, and the world laughs with you.
Snore, and you sleep alone!

Overheard at a convention:
Laughter is the jam on the toast of life.
It makes it easier to swallow; it tastes good;
and it sure keeps life from being so dry.

❀

Humor is to life what shock absorbers
are to an automobile.

❀

A smile is a curve that can set a lot of things straight.

The most important piece of luggage is,
and will remain, a joyful heart.

❀

The most lost day of all is
the one in which we do not laugh.

"How fat can we be and still be jolly?"

5

HEALTH

(Is This Covered by Medicare?)

Statistics prove that a large percent of our concerns are health related. Today, we are more involved with nutrition and physical fitness than ever before.

✚

Mark Twain once said,
"I am an old man and have known a great
many troubles; but most of them never happened."

✚

Wife to overweight husband who continues to stay
in bent-over position after having tied shoes:
"What's wrong, honey? Did you lose something?"
Husband: "No, it's such an effort getting down,
I think I'll polish 'em, too."

The Twenty-Third Pound

My appetite is my shepherd; I always want.
It maketh me sit down and stuff myself.
It leadeth me to my refrigerator repeatedly.
It leadeth me in the path of Burger King for a Whopper.
It destroyeth my shape.
Yea, though I knoweth I gaineth, I will not stop eating,
For the food tasteth so good.
The ice cream and cookies; they comfort me.
When the table is spread before me, it exciteth me,
For I knoweth that I soon shall dig in.
As I filleth my plate continuously,
My clothes runneth smaller.

Surely bulges and weight shall
follow me
all the days of my life,
And I shall be fat forever.

Old age is when knees buckle but belts won't.

✚

The computer salesman was frustrated when,
trying to sell an obese retiree a laptop computer,
the customer's wife caustically asked,
"Where would you put it?"

Two Medicare patients are in a doctor's waiting room. With a sigh of resignation, one says: "Well, I figure from here on in, it's maintenance all the way."

The doctor's parting comment: "Anything new in the way you feel...is most likely a symptom."

✚

A man's health can be judged by which he takes two at a time: pills or stairs.

In my favorite Peanuts cartoon, Snoopy appears
lying on his back, musing:
"I can hear my heart beating,
I can hear my stomach growling,
I can hear my teeth grinding and my joints creaking.
My body's so noisy, I can't sleep."

✚

"Oh, my gosh! It's the truant officer from the exercise class!"

While dining in a posh restaurant in a resort area, an immaculately groomed older matron whispered to her husband. He didn't respond but continued to eat.

He: "Speak up, Mildred, I can't hear you."
She: "Look at me. Now, tell me, where is my filet?
Six o'clock or twelve o'clock on my plate?"
He: "I'm not going to tell you.
Put on your darn glasses."
She: "I will not. You won't wear your hearing aid!"

✚

"*There goes the postman with the Medicare supplement information.*"

One Sunday morning, I shared the pew with a charming older couple. Each wore glasses and each had a hymnal. As we began to sing, I realized they were not going to share. He needed an extension of his arms, and she looked as though she was inspecting a diamond. I didn't know the words, so I hummed.

Have churches considered a larger print for hymnals?

✛

Years may wrinkle the skin, but to give up
interest wrinkles the soul.
—*General Douglas McArthur*

✚

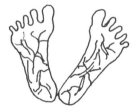

If God had to give a woman wrinkles,
He might at least have put them on
the soles of her feet.

Young at heart—slightly older in other places.

✚

A child's definition:
My memory is the thing I forget with.

"Do you think there'll be enough room when we all breathe?"

*Hanging in my kitchen and done in
cross-stitch by my niece, Laura Thomas:*

I like my bifocals
My dentures fit me fine
My hearing aid is perfect
But, Lordy, how I miss my mind!

✦

When your memory goes, forget it!

✚

"We do not take naps in the daytime unless the grandchildren are here."

6

IT'S GRAND TO BE GRAND
(God's Compensation for Old Age)

When we join the wonderful world of grandparents, we realize for the first time what we missed in our children. I was autographing in a department store when an older gentleman handed me a copy of my first book, *It's Fun at Grandmother's House,* and said, "Mrs. Scott, I was not a good father. I had to be away most of the time. I missed my children's childhood. Thank God for my second chance."

Someone once said that aging has a tendency to make us "set in our ways." We don't just consciously make this decision. It happens without the usual interruptions young ones give to our lives. Grandchildren are our second chance to love, to enjoy, to get out of our ruts!

My late father was very proud of his three daughters, and one day was complimented on his three *granddaughters.* He gave his assurance that they were his daughters. The older gentleman smiled and remarked, "The Lord must have smiled on you."
Politely, my father inquired,
"How many children do you have?"
His response, "Just ten."
Without any hesitation, my father remarked,
"The Lord really laughed on you."

With the gift of our grandchildren, He really did laugh on us, for they are special blessings in our lives.

Parents today are so eager to buy the perfect toy for their children. This ad caught the attention of all subscribers: Guaranteed to amuse any child. Absolutely safe. No need to wind. No batteries required. Portable. Can adjust to any area. For detailed information, dial: 1-800-GRANDPARENTS.

I may not be rich and famous, but I do have priceless grandchildren.

I keep a few examples of my Jamie's "art work" on my refrigerator door. I never realized how lonely a refrigerator door can be until I visited a friend with no grandchildren. Her door was filled with doctors' appointments and one square dancing reminder.

I really think her children should consider that naked refrigerator door when they decide "career, not family."

Things Our Grandchildren Say

*The most flattering comment from a grandchild was
shared by a good friend:*

Baby-sitting a four-year-old can be a very physical
experience. Having played with most of Whitney's
active games, Grandfather suggested some quiet play.
A very determined Whitney wanted to continue.
After a while, he commented, "I'm sure your other
Grandfather doesn't play *all* the games *all* the time." Her
quick response: "I know, Grampy. You see, he doesn't
play with children—he's all grown up."

"Granddaddy, does a chairman of the board like one or two lumps?"

"She's not old! My Granny only wears glasses to keep our baby from punching out her eyes!"

"Grandparents never say, 'We'll have to see about it later!' They do it now!"

A grandmother was bragging that her
grandchild could count backwards.
When asked, "Did you learn that in school?"
he replied, "No, I watch the microwave."

"Grandmothers need more hugs than mothers."

A grandmother and grandchild were looking at some old black and white photographs. Accustomed to only color prints, the grandchild remarked, "Nana, I like the world in color. It must have been awful when everything was in black and white."

Upon returning home after visiting grandmother,
a little girl told her mother about
all the chores she did for her nan.
The mother asked what she
was paid for all that hard work.
The child replied,
"My grandma pays me attention."

7

REFLECTIONS

(It's Later Than You Think)

My very favorite quote is a Yiddish proverb:
Old age to the unlearned is winter;
to the learned, it is the harvest.

～

God gave us memories so that we might
have roses in December.
–*J. M. Barrie*

~

That the birds of worry can
fly above your head,
this you cannot change;
but that they should build
nests in your hair,
this you can prevent!

Don't regret growing older; it is a privilege denied many.

～

The best way to grow old is not to be in a hurry about it.

～

On a plaque in Berta's kitchen:
"I am not afraid of tomorrow,
for I have seen yesterday, and I love today."

A man is getting older when he:
...is warned to slow down by a doctor
instead of a policeman.
...wants to see how long his car will last
instead of how fast it will go.

~

Youth is for learning
Middle age is for doing
Old age is for enjoying.

Old age isn't so bad
when you consider the alternative.
—*Maurice Chevalier*

~

Wife reading husband's will, asks:
"Are you sure you want your funeral at 2:00 A.M.?"
He: "I'm sure. Then you'll find out just how
many friends we *really* have."

I like to give advice
since I am too old to set a bad example.

❧

May your igloo be warm
May your lantern have oil
May you find that peace for your heart.
—*Eskimo proverb*

This bit of prose by Robert Hastings says it all.
When it appeared in Ann Landers's Newsday *column, its effect was overwhelming.*
All the "get around to its" were moved to the front burner.
Trips were taken, relationships were healed, decisions were made.

The Station

Tucked away in our subconscious minds is an idyllic vision.
We see ourselves on a long, long trip that almost spans the continent.
We're traveling by passenger train; and out the windows we drink in the
passing scene of cars on nearby highways, of children waving at a crossing,
of cattle grazing on a distant hillside, of smoke pouring from a power plant,
of row upon row of corn and wheat, of flatlands and valleys, of mountains
and rolling hillsides, of city skylines and village halls, of biting winter and
blazing summer and cavorting spring and docile fall.

But, uppermost in our minds, is the final destination.
On a certain day, at a certain hour, we will pull into the station.
There will be bands playing and flags waving.

And, once we get there, so many wonderful dreams will come true. So many wishes will be fulfilled, and so many pieces of our lives finally will be neatly fitted together like a completed jigsaw puzzle. How restlessly we pace the aisles, damning the minutes for loitering... waiting, waiting, waiting for the station.

However, sooner or later, we must realize there is no one station, no one place to arrive at once and for all. The true joy of life is the trip. The station is only a dream. It finally outdistances us.

"When we reach the station, that will be it!" we cry. Translated, it means, "When I'm 18, that will be it! When I buy a new Mercedes-Benz 450SL, that will be it! When I put the last kid through college, that will be it! When I have paid off the mortgage, that will be it! When I win a promotion, that will be it! When I reach the age of retirement, that will be it! I shall live happily ever after!"

Unfortunately, once we get "it," then "it" disappears.
The station somehow hides itself at the end of an endless track.

"Relish the moment" is a good motto,
especially when coupled with Psalm 118:24:
"This is the day which the Lord hath made;
we will rejoice and be glad in it."
It isn't the burdens of today that drive men mad.
Rather, it is regret over yesterday or fear of tomorrow.
Regret and fear are twin thieves who would rob us of today.

So, stop pacing the aisles and counting the miles.
Instead, climb more mountains, eat more ice cream, go barefoot oftener,
swim more rivers, watch more sunsets, laugh more, and cry less.
Life must be lived as we go along.
The station will come soon enough.

~

Prayer for the Retiree

Lord, thou knowest better than I would know myself that
I am growing older and that someday I shall be old.
Keep me from the fatal habit of thinking I must expound
on every subject and on every occasion.
Release me from craving to straighten out everybody's affairs.
Make me thoughtful but not moody, helpful but not bossy.
With my vast store of wisdom, it seems a pity not to use it all;
but thou knowest, Lord, that I want a few friends at the end.

Keep my mind free from recital of endless details,
give me wings to get to the point.
Seal my lips on my aches and pains.
They are increasing, and love of rehearsing them is
becoming sweeter as the years go by.
I dare not ask for grace to enjoy the tales of others' pains,
but help me to endure with patience.

I dare not ask for improved memory but for growing humility
and a lessening of cocksureness when my memory
seems to clash with the memories of others.
Teach me the glorious lesson that, occasionally,
I could be mistaken.
Keep me reasonably sweet—I do not want to be a saint—
some of them are so hard to live with;
but a sour old person is one of the crowning works of the devil.

Give me the ability to find unexpected talents in people
and to see good things in unexpected places.
And give me, Lord, the grace to say so.

∽

*After reading this bit of prose I changed my salutation from
"How are you?" to "So good to see you, isn't it a wonderful day?"*

Everyday is a wonderful day, so enjoy!

Notes to pages 16-17:
1. Barbara Cartland, *The Atlanta Journal–The Atlanta Constitution.*
2. Art Linkletter, *The Atlanta Journal–The Atlanta Constitution.*
3. Alice Faye, *50 Plus*, January 1988.
4. George Burns, "Newsmakers," *The Atlanta Journal–The Atlanta Constitution.*

About the author:

Blackie Scott, a native of Virginia, is an entertainment consultant, and is active on the national speaking circuit, speaking on various humorous subjects including "Retire and Rejoice." She and her husband live in Atlanta; they have one daughter and three grandchildren. She is the author of three other books, *It's Fun to Entertain, It's Fun at Grandmother's House,* and *Corporate Success.*

About the illustrator:

Bill Johnson has taught art at Georgia State University and the Atlanta College of Art. A graphic designer and illustrator, he is also a frequently exhibited painter known for his vibrant watercolors. He lives in Atlanta.